Cambodian Adventures

Cambodian Adventures

Donna Vann

CF4·K

Published in 2009
by
Christian Focus Publications,
Geanies House, Fearn, Tain,
Ross-shire, IV20 1TW,
Great Britain

Cover design by Daniel van Straaten
Cover illustration by Graham Kennedy
Other illustrations by Fred Apps
Printed by MPG Books Ltd, Bodmin, Cornwall

Scripture quotations are taken from the Holy Bible,
New Living Translation, copyright ©1996.
Used by permission of Tyndale House Publishers, Inc.,
Wheaton, Illinois 60189. All rights reserved.

Dedicated with much love to David and Laura.
Thank you for allowing me to use your experiences
of the Cambodian people and culture in this book.

Contents

Come with us to Cambodia

It is the end of Christmas day. I curl up in bed under a mosquito net, making sure the white netting is securely tucked under the mattress on all sides. This is our first day of a two-week visit to Cambodia, and I want to record it in my journal before drifting off to a well-earned sleep.

All is quiet except for the gentle thrum of the ceiling fan and the chuck-chuck of geckoes which live in the thatched roof of our beach cottage. Suddenly the air throbs with amplified sound. What on earth can it be? We hear music and loud wailing noises which might be singing. Eventually we figure out that a mammoth karaoke has been set up on the beach just outside our guest house. I'd hoped for a peaceful night, but no chance! Karaoke is popular in Cambodia and this is obviously going to be the biggest event of the season in the local village. Oh well, at least I'll be able to stay awake to write in my journal.

Cambodia, tucked between Thailand and Vietnam, is slightly smaller than the UK in area but with only about 14 million people. Along with Laos and Myanmar, these five countries southeast of China are known as Southeast Asia.

We have come to visit Dave and Laura, our son and his wife, who are Christian workers in Cambodia. Many of the stories and facts in this book are taken from their Cambodian letters and blog. As you read, you will travel to real places in this fascinating country. You will meet a few wild creatures, some which they saw and others which they were glad not to encounter! You will be introduced to unique Cambodian people and learn about the challenge of being a Christian in this mostly Buddhist country.

You'll find out what fried spiders taste like, and why many Cambodians look so young. Your tour will include one of the largest inland lakes in the world and the remains of an ancient civilisation. You'll learn why it's dangerous to step off the beaten path in some parts of the country, and why some children don't know when their birthdays are. You may even get to see some dolphins!

Even though many people in Cambodia know very little about the one true God, you will discover that God has not forgotten Cambodia. He is at work here in surprising ways. So come along, and don't forget your insect repellent!

Who Drives the Best Vehicle?

We are riding in a van heading into the city of Phnom Penh, where Dave and Laura live. Our first impression is of a fairly modern city, with wide streets and well-kept buildings. But it doesn't take long before we notice a big difference: the traffic!

All kinds of vehicles throng the streets of Phnom Penh, which is the capital city of about a million inhabitants. There seem to be no particular rules of the road. Everyone weaves in and out in what looks like an elaborate dance. I want to cover my eyes, but then decide I'd rather know if we are about to have a crash!

First there are the lordly SUV's, kings of the roads. All other drivers give way before these important four-wheel-drive vehicles. Then come other expensive cars like Mercedes; they take second place on the streets, followed by taxis, vans, trucks and ordinary cars. Next in line are the *tuk-tuks*, which are roofed carriages pulled by a driver riding a motorcycle. The passengers sit on benches facing each other. It's a fun way to ride, though often bumpy, as many streets are not paved.

Tuk-tuks are followed by *motos* – motorcycles which have room for a passenger or two clinging on behind the driver. Then come the *cyclos*: this looks like a bicycle but has two wheels in front, topped by a comfortable seat for one passenger. Down at the bottom of the list are normal bicycles, then people pushing wooden hand-carts, and finally pedestrians. Being on the road in Cambodia is like being in a giant scary game of rock, paper, scissors – who is the strongest?

Dave gives us some advice to remember for later, when we'll be walking through the city: 'When you're crossing the street, don't cross at the crosswalk. No one will stop for you. The best way to cross is by weaving at a steady pace through the moving traffic. If you run, or if you stop suddenly, you're likely to be hit!'

Cambodia is called a kingdom and has a king who lives in a grand palace, although a prime minister runs the government. On our first day we're impressed by the wealth of this city when we visit the vast royal palace compound. At the Silver Pagoda we walk on a floor made up of 5,000 silver tiles and gaze at statues made of gold and diamonds. That evening we leave our hotel and take a tuk-tuk (try saying that three times quickly!) to meet Dave and Laura. Jouncing along in the tuk-tuk, we experience a different side of Phnom Penh: dark streets with rubble and potholes lurking everywhere; street corners crowded with vendors selling hot food or lottery tickets or doing roadside bicycle repair.

Finally we reach the Young Life Centre, a white building behind a walled courtyard which is crowded with teenagers. Dave and Laura help out with this Christian club, where young people can learn about Jesus and grow in their faith. We leave our shoes with dozens of others on the porch, and join the teens who cram

into the small hall, sitting on the polished tile floor. After some enthusiastic singing, Dave gives a talk in English which is translated into Khmer, the main language spoken in Cambodia.

After the meeting we walk again through dark dusty streets. We come upon a huge barbecue grill set up beside the road. Our mouths water at the appetizing smells of roasting meat. A woman holding long metal tongs perches on a stool behind the grill. She wears gloves and hat to protect her from the heat and sparks which sail up into the night sky. Her plump cheeks glow in the firelight as she turns pieces of sizzling chicken or pork. We join the crowd and buy our supper to take home.

Back at Dave and Laura's apartment, while we eat our grilled chicken and fresh boiled sweetcorn, they explain about the two vastly different views of Phnom Penh. On the one hand are the average residents of the city. Most are Cambodian nationals (called *Khmer*) who might be street vendors, moto taxi drivers, shopkeepers, street cleaners, builders, beggars or businessmen. They will probably hold down more than one job to support family members who live in distant villages. Their homes might be wooden shacks on stilts or simple apartments. They probably eat Cambodian food sold on the street corners, including such delicacies as deep-fried sparrows!

A few things stand out as important for the average Khmer in the city: a mobile phone, a television, a car. They might even sell the furniture in their homes, so they can buy one of these signs of status. If they manage to buy a car, they will often park it in the front room of their house! Think about yourself: what in your life is that important? Is there something you would sell everything to get? How about getting to know God – is that something you would give up everything for?

Then there is the other side of Phnom Penh. The thousands of foreign workers living here seem wealthy by comparison with the locals. They belong to groups who have come in to help develop the country of Cambodia. Many of these foreigners work at one job in an office, and eat western-style food available at cafes and restaurants around the city. They drive SUV's through the crowded streets. They probably live in a large apartment or mansion on the outskirts of the city.

Dave and Laura didn't want to isolate themselves from the Khmer and only be friends with other people like themselves. So they made a point of living in a Cambodian neighbourhood and trying to get to know their neighbours. They knew this was what Jesus did. He spent time with ordinary people, those whom others ignored or looked down on.

Their first months in Cambodia were not easy. The Khmer get up very early – by five in the morning everyone is bustling around and dogs are barking. Fortunately their apartment was not near one of the open sewer canals that run through parts of the city, so the smells weren't too bad. Whenever Dave and Laura left their apartment and went out on the street, people would stare at them. It was tough being looked upon as the rich westerners.

But as they began to learn the language, people were able to get to know them. One friendly woman named Sambat from across the street invited Dave and Laura to her wedding. As Dave and Laura learned more of the Khmer language, they were gradually able to tell Sambat about Jesus. This Buddhist woman didn't always get what they were saying, yet she responded to care and friendship from these foreigners.

That's also what happened to Phola, a young woman in the Young Life group. It all began when she was invited by a friend to attend a Young Life meeting on a Saturday night. She met people who seemed to have peace and joy in their lives. Gradually she came to understand that this grew out of their knowing God. Her new friends explained to her that Jesus, God's Son, died a horrible death so that she, Phola, might be able to be totally forgiven for every wrong thing she had ever done.

Phola came from a Buddhist family, but her religion did not make a difference to her life in the way these Christians spoke of. She understood that if she took the step of trusting in Jesus, he would forgive her completely. She also knew that becoming a follower of Jesus would cause problems with her family. Yet she could not turn away. She sensed that knowing Jesus was worth whatever it cost, and she gave her life to him.

Trouble flared up right away. Phola's father, a respected local Buddhist leader, was angry over her newfound faith. He ordered her to leave home. 'You have betrayed us!' he said. When Phola became a Christian, it was like turning her back on her family and even on her culture. Although she has been allowed to return home, Phola faces a difficult time of trying to help her family understand and trust her again.

Thousands of Cambodian Christians like Phola have a challenge. They want to show respect to Cambodian values and traditions, but their main goal is to live as followers of Jesus. Often this causes tension in this Buddhist country. Many Christians have been cast off by their families, but at the same time they have gained a priceless treasure.

Jesus said the kingdom of heaven is like a treasure hidden in a field: someone found it, then sold everything he owned to buy that field. He also said it was like a pearl of great value. A merchant sold everything he had, in order to buy this pearl. (Matthew 13:44-46).

Have you found the kingdom of heaven? If you have put your trust in Jesus, asking forgiveness for whatever you have done wrong, then you belong to God's kingdom. You can count on him to help you know how to live each day, and to take you to be with him in heaven when you die. If you have never done this, why not talk to him about it?

But to all who believed him (Jesus) and accepted him, he gave the right to become children of God. (John 1:12)

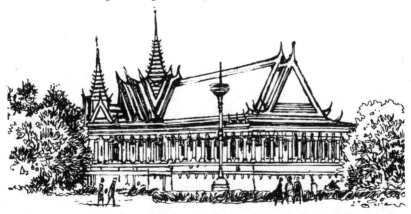

Fried Spiders and Village Adventures

We are about to leave Phnom Penh after several days to make the journey north to visit the ancient temples of Angkor. Dave and Laura's friend Jun will travel with us in a hired twelve-seater van. Jun lives with them in the city, but wants to visit his family in a small village which is on our way.

I start to wonder where we might take our rest stops on the trip. In Cambodia, this is something you need to think about. A few days before, when we travelled three hours to the coast, there was only one place along the way with a toilet. And that was in a hut in someone's back garden!

Laura smiles at my worry. 'You'll just have to learn to go in the fields, the way I have.' She tells of a time when she and Dave stayed in a village overnight. When they arrived, she was shown the proper place in the fields. Their hostess announced to the whole village, 'Laura is going to the field!'

In the middle of the night she had to go again, so she made her way out of the hut in the darkness. Several lively puppies started jumping up on her, wanting to play. Laura tried desperately not to wake the mother dog, which would then bark and wake the whole village. Finally she found what she thought would be a good spot, but then she realised she was in the cattle pen! Fortunately, the huge animals were sleeping.

With all our toilet stops planned, our van driver weaves his way in and out of the hectic city traffic. It doesn't seem like he's done much driving before, so we're thankful when we finally reach the open road. On each side of the road we see rice fields called *paddies* in the flat landscape, now mostly dry and brown. Later in the year they will be wet and green with newly sprouted rice.

Occasionally we glimpse a cow or two in a field, but these are not plump dairy cows. Cambodian cows are so scrawny that all cow's milk has to be imported into the country, at a high price.

About two hours into our journey, Jun asks the driver to pull over at a service station. I notice Jun buys something, maybe some sweets, which he carries in a small paper bag. Back in the van, he rips open his bag and shows us his treat: three giant black tarantula spiders, crispy fried! I decide to look out the window as he first breaks off the crunchy legs and eats them. Then he drains the pus out of the body and pops that into his mouth (as the others told me later). I hope you are not reading this any time close to Christmas, because the spider body has the texture of stuffing that goes into the Christmas turkey. The spider legs have a charcoal flavour.

Not only spiders but also cockroaches, worms and other insects are considered delicious snacks here. You see big barrels of them on display in the markets. Well, why not? Insect life is plentiful – they provide protein at no cost. In our western society, if we see a roach we get out the bug spray. Maybe we should grab an insect net instead. Grasshopper stew, anyone?

A little while later, the van turns down a deeply rutted dirt road and drops us off at the village where Jun's family lives. We walk along the dusty road bordered with tall palm trees. Soon we see weathered grey houses raised up on poles, lining the road on both sides. Some of these one-room houses are thatched with palm, while others have wooden or tin roofs. A simple wooden ladder on the outside leads up to the one door of each house. Many people recognise Jun and greet him. They look puzzled to see us – white people are a rare sight in this place.

Some of the village houses have another tiny house on a pole out front. These look like fancy bird houses, painted bright colours, some with little steps going up into the door. Laura explains that these are not bird houses, but spirit houses. Many people believe that when someone in their family dies, their spirit will want to stay near the family. Relatives build these little houses and put offerings of bananas or other fruit on the ledge, so that the spirits will stay happy and treat them well. When bad things happen, they believe it is because they have angered the ancestor spirits in some way.

Jun's family is not Buddhist like most of those in the village, but Christian. They know their dead ancestors did not turn into spirits. They don't have a spirit house, because they know that God does not live in houses made by carpenters. God is not weak, so that he might need steps to get up into his little house. He also doesn't want us to live in fear of him, giving him gifts to keep him from getting angry with us.

Just the opposite: God loves us so much, that even before we were born, he sent his Son Jesus to live on earth. He did this to show people what God is really like. He is kind and loving, wanting every person to get to know him and follow him. But more than that, God sent Jesus to save us. Jesus was crucified on a cross, but God brought him back to life. This death was the payment for every wrong thing that we have thought, said or done. Jesus was punished, so we don't have to be. This opened the way for people to get to know God.

If you would like to know him, all you need to do is ask. Simply ask his forgiveness and thank him for sending Jesus to save you. If you aren't sure what to say, just tell him what's on your mind and heart. He will understand, no matter how you say it. Or if you want to, you could say something like this:

Dear God, thank you for sending your son, Jesus. Thank you that he died on the cross for all the wrong things I have thought and said and done. Please forgive me and let me be in your family forever. Help me to be the kind of person you want me to be. Thank you for answering my prayer.

If you have put your trust in Jesus, then *you* become the house God lives in! His Spirit comes to make his home in you, to help you to know God better and to become what he longs for you to be.

In the village we make our way to the home of Jun's brother. His sister-in-law welcomes us and invites us to rest on the low platform of wooden slats beneath her house. This is a good place to sit outdoors and be protected from rain or sun. After a while, Jun's mother invites us to come inside her house. We climb the steep ladder and enter the one-room house, where she has placed straw mats on the floor for us to sit. A simple curtain divides the front of the room from the sleeping area. The only item in the room is a car battery – the village has no electricity, so batteries are used to run lights at night.

After chatting with Jun's mum, with Jun translating, we climb back down the ladder. The sun is setting. How are all six of us going to get to another village a few kilometres away, where we are staying the night? There are no cars here. No problem; someone finds a man who owns a small shallow wooden cart drawn by a pony. We squash into the cart, and are off – slowly –feeling a bit sorry for the poor pony!

We may look funny all packed together in the pony cart but, except for our pale skins, we are a normal sight for transport in rural Cambodia. As well as carts, there are vans which act like buses, collecting people from the side of the road. Some of these people may have a live chicken strapped to their wrist, to keep it from escaping. No one worries too much if the van is full. Probably a twelve-seater van can actually seat thirty people all squashed together, and then you can get another twenty or so on the roof.

If you want to carry a couple of pigs to market, you can tie them up behind you on your motorcycle. We pass vans with live chickens tied to the roof, and see two people on a motorcycle carrying a huge sheet of glass. The idea is, if you have anything or anyone you need to transport, and you have any type of vehicle with wheels, you can make it work!

That night we stop over at an 'eco-village' built to show westerners what life in a Cambodian village is like. After a meal which includes sour melon stew, we are entertained with traditional dancing by a local Christian youth group. Then we climb the ladders into our one-room houses and get ready for bed by the light powered from a car battery. We make sure our mosquito nets are tucked securely in all around the edges of our mats, then turn the light out by nine, as we know we will have an early start.

Crowing roosters wake us the next morning. In the pale light before dawn we see children cycling down the road heading for school. Soon we are dressed and all pile into pony carts (two this time). Our first stop is the local market, which is heaving with people at this early hour. It smells of dust and frying food. We eat a breakfast of rice with meat at an incredibly grubby stall, then take a tour of the market. The breakfast tasted yummy but our stomachs are turning now as we see the huge head of a pig on a wooden slab, with its intestines laid out neatly beside it.

Unless they are working at the market, the local women will come here to buy food every morning and perhaps in the evening as well. Their houses have no fridges or freezers – everything is bought fresh, and will be eaten that day.

In general, village women spend their whole day caring for house and home and children. They are often up by five am. First they sweep their house and the area in front, then cook breakfast for the family. This may be rice porridge with bits of meat or fish. Or they might prepare rice with some sweet marinated pork, finely chopped spring onions and a mixture of pickled vegetables.

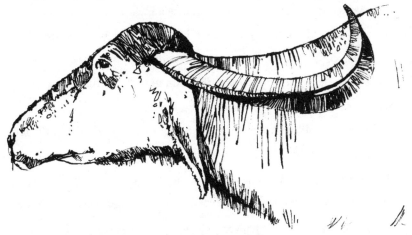

Most of the village men are farmers, either of rice or fruit such as mangoes. Others are mechanics or fishermen. Often men move to the city to find work, only coming home occasionally to see their families and give them money.

If a man stays in the village, he will most likely be involved in rice farming. Villagers may own one small rice paddy or else work as tenant farmers for a landowner. Women and children also work in the rice paddies during planting and harvest.

Water buffalo are a common sight in rural Cambodia. They often have the task of ploughing up fields for planting. These sturdy creatures with their thick, wide horns are useful in the soggy rice paddies. Cattle prefer not to wade in water, but the water buffalo seem designed for the job. Their large padded hooves are ideal for sloshing through squishy mud. Although they weigh about a thousand kilos and look scary, they are actually gentle. You often see children riding them through the fields.

After the fields are ploughed and flooded, workers plant rice seedlings by hand. These grow quickly in the hot sun and moisture, but so do weeds. Aquatic plants such as duckweed thrive, taking over the space needed by the rice plants. These weeds are then pulled up by hand – tedious, backbreaking work.

Rice farmers are often paid less than fifty pence a day, working during the rainy season. There is little work during the five months of dry season. They have to save up enough money or enough rice to feed their families during that time.

People eat rice every day in Southeast Asia. The Cambodian government is trying to help farmers produce more rice per area. If they irrigate properly, in other words if they control the water levels in the fields, they can get two crops a year instead of one. Some farmers breed fish that eat the insects which destroy the plants. When the fish get bigger the farmer's family can eat them.

The 'fish counter' is the last stop on our tour of the market. Actually it's not a counter, but a very smelly area where women squat on the ground, gutting and cleaning fish. We decide not to buy any. Our village tour guide then takes us to a field on the edge of the village, where we watch rice being threshed with a machine resembling a portable steam engine. She points out a nearby palm tree and asks, 'Who wants to climb it?'

It looks hard, scrambling up a tall tree trunk, gripping on with your bare feet and hands. And it would be – except there just happens to be a slender pole right next to the tree, with places to put your hands and feet. We tourists get to do it the easy way!

After our climb, the guide gives us small cups of palm juice to drink. If anyone offers you palm juice, my advice is, don't take it. It tastes like pureed cabbage.

Then we travel in our pony carts to a school, where small children in uniform are learning the Khmer alphabet. The teacher holds up a card with each letter, and the children chant it aloud. I think all the letters look alike, and when strung together look like caterpillars! Here is *Kingdom of Cambodia* in Khmer:

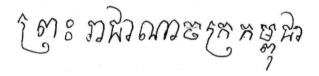

Our tour ends at an open shed holding huge looms for weaving. This is the Khmer Life project, one of many in Cambodia which trains craft workers and helps them to get a fair price for what they produce. The charity helps villagers in the province of Kompong Thom to break out of poverty.

Chandon is one such person. Even as a young girl, she had to work hard to raise vegetables and take them to market in Phnom Penh. Her parents were both ill and could not help much. If she couldn't sell enough vegetables, Chandon would also make a little money by picking through rubbish at the city dump to find things to sell. Many people in the cities make a living like this.

When Chandon was sixteen both her parents died. What would she do? Then her aunt who lived in a village in Kompong Thom province arranged for Chandon to come and live with her. She arrived with no possessions and no money. How would she live? Before long, her aunt signed her up for weaving training at the nearby Khmer Life Centre.

Chandon did so well on the course that she was offered a permanent job at the Centre. Although she still misses her parents, today she says life is good. She has decided to become a Christian and attends a local church. Chandon smiles as she talks of her new job, her new friends and her new faith. 'I now know that there's a spiritual life that I need to look after,' she says.

Although Chandon did not know it, God had been watching over her all those years when she struggled to feed her family. She did not have a chance to know him then, but later when she learned about God and about Jesus, who gave his life for her, Chandon was ready to respond.

God does not need to be kept happy with gifts, as many people in Cambodia believe. Instead of demanding gifts, God is generous and loves to give gifts to others. Long ago, before you were born, God knew that you would be alive today, and he wants to get to know you. He is waiting for you to trust him, just as he waited for Chandon. Does he have first place in your life? Have you told him that you want to belong to him and live for him each day? There is only one gift God would love to have: you!

The eyes of the Lord search the whole earth in order to strengthen those whose hearts are fully committed to him. (2 Chronicles 16:9)

Water Everywhere!

'Stop that!' Diep scolds her younger brother Binh. 'If we fall in the lake, my books will get soaked!'

Binh giggles, but he stops rocking the boat. The two children continue paddling their tiny craft through the dirty waters of the Tonle Sap lake. They still have another kilometre to go before they reach their school.

Diep and Binh live on this vast lake that looks more like an ocean, and their school is on another part of the lake. This doesn't mean that their house and school are on the land next to the lake. On the Tonle Sap, some of the villages and schools are floating on the waters of the lake! Everyone has to get around in boats. Children climb into washtubs and paddle out to meet up with their friends.

The dry season in Cambodia lasts from November through April. Little or no rain falls during those months, and Tonle Sap lake is only about a metre in depth. The waters of the Tonle Sap flow down to join up with the Mekong River and on to the sea.

But during the rainy season from May to October, something surprising happens. The heavy rains of the monsoon season plus melting snow from the distant Himalayas drain into the Mekong. The overflow pours into the Tonle Sap branch of the Mekong. The result is that instead of heading to the sea, as any normal river would, this river reverses its flow and fills Tonle Sap lake. The lake swells to nearly three times its dry-season size.

That is the time when Diep and Binh's parents and the rest of the people in their village move their houses. Some buildings rest on floating platforms so they can be easily towed by boat from one part of the lake to another, as the water rises or declines. Small houses built on the lake's edge are hoisted on the back of a truck and driven to another spot, as the water levels change. That way, the village will always remain near the shore of the lake.

It might sound romantic, living on a floating house on the Tonle Sap, the largest lake in Southeast Asia. Tourists love to visit the floating village where Diep and Binh and their parents and grandparents have always lived. The family is ethnic Vietnamese, as are many of the lake-dwellers. Their father makes his living fishing in this mammoth lake.

But he is not allowed to fish wherever he wants. Large areas have been fenced off by commercial fisheries, keeping the poor fishermen out. Diep and Binh's floating one-room house has no electricity. There is no pipe bringing in fresh water. The family doesn't even have a toilet. Everything ends up in the lake! You can imagine what it smells like, especially in the dry season.

Not long ago, the government asked the villagers if they wanted to keep living on the water, or move to dry land. Most said they wanted to live on the land, with running water and lights

and toilets, as long as they could still fish. If the village moves to dry land, Binh and Diep will be able to walk to school instead of having to row in a boat.

As they walk through the jungle on their way to school, the children will very likely see monkeys. Most common are the small grey monkeys which are very friendly, scampering across the road with little fear of humans. Cambodia is also home to several rare species of monkey, such as the black-shanked douc langur and the yellow-cheeked crested gibbon. Binh and Diep will have to stare very hard into the thick jungle foliage to catch sight of one of these. Many rare monkeys are in danger of dying out as their native forests are chopped down.

Walking along a jungle path to school might sound less dangerous than rowing, but Diep and Binh will have to watch out for deadly snakes, of which there are several in Cambodia. One is the tree-dwelling green tree pit viper. It will only attack if you provoke it, but it can give you a nasty bite on the face.

The cobra is an aggressive snake which may even enter a house, looking for a rat to eat. When threatened, it will lift its head and spread out its hood. The snake thinks this makes it look dangerous, which it does! A cobra bite may be fatal if not treated right away.

The best thing to do if you encounter a cobra is to get out of its way, and give it plenty of room to escape.

Then there are pythons, which can grow up to three metres long and squeeze their prey to death. They can even kill and eat something as large as a goat.

Perhaps the most dangerous reptile for Diep and Binh would be the Malayan pit viper, a bad-tempered snake with long fangs. Its triangular brown markings help it to blend into the ground, where it lurks hunting for food. Villagers think nothing of walking through the fields barefoot or wearing open sandals. They may step right on a viper before they see it. Naturally, the snake doesn't like that and it will bite. However if the bite gets treated right away, it may not be fatal.

I assume you will not be walking through the fields and forests of Cambodia barefoot! But just in case, here's what to do for snakebite:

- Have the victim lie down and keep still.
- Put a tight bulky bandage on the bite and make a splint to hold it steady.
- Keep the bitten part of the body lower than the heart.
- Remove all jewellery.
- Get the person to a hospital or clinic as soon as possible.
- Do not try to kill the snake. Dead snakes and even severed snake heads may still 'bite' several hours after death, due to muscle contractions.

You may think it's silly not to wear sturdy shoes, if there are so many snakes around. But in the hot Cambodian climate, sandals or flip-flops are the most comfortable footwear. Also, when you enter a home, you always remove your shoes. So it makes sense to be able to slip out of your shoes easily.

Perhaps you don't live in a country with so many poisonous snakes. But no matter where you live, you may be in danger from an enemy as clever and good at hiding as a snake. I'm talking about the enemy of Christians, known as Satan or the Devil. The Bible tells us that this enemy accuses Christians before God day and night.

God does not pay any attention when Satan points the finger in blame at you. There is nothing that he holds against you now, if you have trusted in Jesus to save you. It's important to be on guard against Satan's tricks. This enemy of God will say you are bad through and through, and that God doesn't love you. The truth is, God loves you much more than even your parents could possibly love you. If you know you've done something wrong, simply ask God to forgive you and thank him that he already has. You don't have to listen to the enemy's lies.

The enemy may also try and persuade you that you don't belong to God any more. But Jesus said that he holds you tightly in his hands, and that no one can steal you away from him. You may not always feel like you belong to him, but you do. Even if you are having a bad day, Jesus has not left you. He promised never to leave anyone who has put their trust in him. You can count on it!

Along with snakes, the weather can be another enemy in Cambodia. During the monsoon months of May through October it rains heavily for part of every day. If you are out walking during the monsoon, it feels like a giant bathtub in the sky has suddenly tipped over. You may think you can keep dry under a raincoat, but it's like trying to keep dry in a swimming pool – a bit tricky! Heavy rains cause up to two-thirds of the farmland in the whole county to be covered by water.

Villagers build their houses on stilts and get around in small boats during the flood season. In the cities, traffic sometimes has to struggle on through deep water. One day during the monsoon, Dave was riding his motorbike near a large market in Phnom Penh when he hit a flooded street. Suddenly, his bike spluttered and died. His only choice was to push it through water up to his waist. Then he realised he was wading through the rubbish and rotten vegetables thrown out from the market. People stood in their doorways and laughed to see the foreigner struggling through high water with bits of carrot and cabbage bobbing around him!

Another water adventure occurred when a faulty water pipe in their apartment burst, spewing gallons of water into the apartment of their neighbours next door. But their landlord wouldn't repair it. This man believes when something like that goes wrong, it is caused by angry spirits. He may have thought, 'Why should I bother to fix the pipe? The angry spirits will only cause it to break again.'

The landlord's belief in spirits had an effect on the way he acted. If you are a believer in Jesus, that should also affect the way you act. For example, when you are in trouble, how do you react? Do you try to ignore the problem? Do you worry and fret? Do you get angry and blame someone else? Do you pray? Which of these do you think would show that you believe in a good God, who loves you very much?

Too much water can cause problems, but water is also a boon for Cambodia. The floods which swamp the fields each year make for a plentiful rice harvest. Fish thrive in the flooded lakes. More than 800 species of fish live in the waters of the Tonle Sap, which supplies three-fourths of all the fish caught in Cambodia.

Water also provides the highlight of the year in the city of Phnom Penh: the Water Festival. This is the time when the waters of the Tonle Sap river turn again and flow down towards the sea. It signals the end of the monsoon and the beginning of the dry season when most weddings will take place. Spectators jam the riverbanks near the meeting point of three mighty rivers, the Mekong, Bassac and Tonle Sap for the annual boat race.

Several hundred rowing teams compete, in long narrow boats crammed with up to a hundred oarsmen in double rows. This is no sedate competition, however. Whistles and drums of the coxswains pierce the air, along with cheers and clapping from the crowds in stands built along the shore. Each team wears shirts in a single bright colour. Some, like the ethnic Chams, row standing, their long plaid skirts looking like pale Scottish kilts. In the excitement

and confusion boats can crash into each other as they dash for the finish line.

About three million people gather on the banks of the Mekong in November to watch these races which celebrate 'the turning of the waters'. But very few make the journey back up the main eastern arm of the Mekong, to the town of Kratie. Those who do are rewarded with a unique sight, one that may not be visible much longer. These are the Irrawady dolphins of Cambodia.

Unlike the common dolphin with its grey skin and pointed snout, Irrawady dolphins have a stubby head and brownish-grey skin. Several small groups known as 'pods' live in the Mekong. They play in the waters, unaware that their existence is threatened.

This year there are less than a hundred Irrawady at Kratie and even dolphin calves are dying.

Fishermen on this part of the Mekong River are being asked to take up chicken farming, in order to keep the dolphins from being trapped in fishing nets. But still the dolphins are dying, perhaps from pollution. Unless the government can figure out a solution, this amazing water creature will soon disappear from Cambodia.

Water has an important place in Cambodia, and also in the Bible. Once when Jesus was at a huge festival in the city of Jerusalem, he stood up and shouted to the crowds, 'If you are thirsty, come to me! If you believe in me, come and drink! For the Scriptures declare that rivers of living water will flow out from within.' (John 7:37-38) Another time, he told a woman who was drawing water from a well, 'If you only knew the gift God has for you and who I am, you would ask me, and I would give you living water.' (John 4:10)

When Jesus spoke of 'living water' he was talking about his Spirit. If you have trusted in Jesus to forgive your sins and give you new life, then you have the Spirit of Jesus living in you. He is often called the Holy Spirit. He comes into your life the moment you give your life to Jesus, and he will never go away.

The Holy Spirit will teach you things Jesus wants you to know, as you read the Bible. This special book is like a letter from God to you. His Spirit will help you to understand it, and make it real in your life.

The Spirit will also help you pray and will guide you in living as God wants, if you will let him. You may not feel as if he is there, but your life will gradually change. By letting the Holy Spirit direct your life, you will show that you are truly a follower of Jesus by the way you live.

For all who are led by the Spirit of God are children of God. (Romans 8.14)

Wonders of the World

'Very nice postcards, Madame, you want to buy?'

The girl holds up a folder of postcards showing the Angkor temples, which we have just toured. She seems about eight years old.

'Look, very nice,' she says, fanning them out so we can see. 'Only one dollar!'

'Don't you have to go to school?' I ask.

'Yes, I go to school. Very nice postcards, only one dollar. You want to buy?'

The ancient city of Angkor in northwest Cambodia is one of the major wonders of the world. Hundreds of years ago, Cambodia was a powerful kingdom with rulers who worshipped the gods of the Hindu religion, and later Buddha. Beginning around 900 AD, these kings built vast temple fortresses to the north of the Tonle Sap lake.

At one time Angkor city was about five times the size of modern-day London and had over a million people, which made it the largest city on earth before the age of machines. In the fifteenth century it was destroyed by Siam (now Thailand) and the capital moved south, to Phnom Penh. Around two million tourists visit Angkor each year.

The most popular of the many temples is called Angkor Wat (*wat* means temple). It is an immense complex built in the twelfth century, with walls one kilometre long and towers rising from the temple 'mountain' in the centre. The Cambodian flag bears the image of the three front towers of Angkor Wat. They remind me of pointy pineapples.

In the centre of Angkor Wat is a small tower with incredibly steep steps. Some of our group decide to risk the climb, but I stay safely on the ground and take photos of them inching their way back down. I am glad that God doesn't ask people to climb up to a special dangerous high place, in order to worship him. We

can worship him wherever we are. At sunset we leave the galleries of Angkor Wat, to the sound of chanting and drums from the Buddhist monks who still worship there.

The next day we tour several other temples. At Preah Khan and Ta Prohm temples we clamber over giant stone blocks and imagine we are explorers who have stumbled upon these ruins rising out of the jungle.

A startling sight at these temples are the tall silk-cotton or *kapok* trees. At first glance they look like something out of a horror film: colossal roots seem to drip like rising bread dough over the temple walls. In some cases the walls are only standing because they are propped up by the giant roots.

Even more spooky is the fact that these roots are invaders. They don't belong to the kapok tree at all. Sometimes a tiny seed of another tree nestles in the top of a kapok. The seed sprouts and spreads, weaving its way around the kapok trunk. As this enemy tree puts out foliage and roots, it gradually squeezes the life out of the kapok underneath, until nothing is left of the original tree. There is only a hollow trunk. The new tree continues to grow and spread its roots around whatever is in its path, even stone walls. It is called a *strangler fig* and I think you'll agree that is a good name for it!

The wood of the strangler fig is so gnarled and twisted that it can't be used for anything. On the other hand, its fruit is good to eat. The hollow trunk of the host tree provides a home for many small creatures of the forest. Also, the strangler offers some amazing photo opportunities! Otherwise, it is mostly a nuisance.

Occasionally the strangler fig gets too strong for the ancient stone, and sections of the temple collapse. With all the tourists swarming over the Angkor temples, plus damage from the weather, it is a challenge to figure out how to preserve these monuments. They need to be protected. The local residents depend on money the tourists bring, for their livelihood.

We did buy postcards from the young girl who asked us, but I am not at all sure that she attended school, in spite of what she said. And I wonder what would have happened to her that evening, if she returned home without having sold enough postcards.

Although most children in Cambodia are in school, they only attend for half a day. They might go early in the morning, just as the sun is rising, and come home at lunchtime. Or, they go to school after lunch and come home in the late afternoon. Each classroom is filled twice a day, and each teacher works hard all day, teaching two groups of children. Each class may have as many as one hundred children.

Many parents can't afford to send their children to school. They have no money to pay bribes to the poor teachers or buy clothes or school supplies. Like the girl I bought postcards from, Cambodian children often have to work at an early age. Many grown-ups were killed in the Khmer Rouge fighting in the 1970's and 1980's, so often children are left without any grandparents or extended family to look after them.

Sometimes even when the children have a family, their parents are so poor that they will sell any of their children who don't bring in money. The children have to go and live with someone else who will make them work very hard.

Can you imagine living with that fear: *If I don't make enough money, my parents might sell me....* I wonder if the postcard girl was scared of this happening. I tried to talk to her, but I soon discovered that she had learned only a few phrases in English, in order to sell her postcards. She did not really speak the language.

Although we didn't learn any more about the children of Angkor, Dave and Laura have been able to meet some of the poor children of Phnom Penh. About 15,000 children live on the streets in that city. Many of them earn a few pennies a day by picking through rubbish in the large city dump. They dig through stinking heaps to find rags, plastic, metal cans and anything else they can sell to 'recyclers'. Then they will set a patch of rubbish on fire to extract any metal, which can also be sold. Many go barefoot and work with bare hands, not knowing or caring that infected needles from the local hospitals are dumped there too. They could catch a horrible disease, but they have to work – they have no choice, if they want to live.

Think about it: how would you feel if you were one of these kids? What did Jesus think about children? Did he think they were important?

Jesus lived at a time when children were not considered important at all. Once some parents brought their children to Jesus so that he could bless them, but Jesus' friends scolded them. They thought he wouldn't want to be bothered. Instead, Jesus took the children in his arms and told off his friends for trying to keep them away.

He even said to the grown-ups that everyone needs to become like a little child, in order to come into the kingdom of heaven. He wants everyone to trust him in a simple, humble way. Even a young child can understand enough to know they want to belong to Jesus.

I imagine that Jesus would say, the wonders of the world are its children. In Cambodia the streets are swarming with kids of all ages. So many are poor and ill. What will their future be?

Yet some people are helping. If you go to a large grassy roundabout in the centre of Phnom Penh at five on a Friday afternoon, you will see a surprising sight. Hoards of ragged children are milling around on the grass. They look eager, as if they are waiting for something exciting to happen.

Suddenly they all start running in one direction, as a big green bus wheels around the corner and parks at the kerb. Children crowd round the door, jostling each other in their eagerness to climb aboard. This is the Hischild bus, where street children can have a shower, have their nails cut and get basic first-aid treatment. The Hischild workers will feed them, play games and tell them Bible stories. The children will also learn about basic health and cleanliness, and get a chance to practice their alphabet and times tables.

Laura and Dave were able to help out occasionally at the bus. One evening Laura saw a tiny girl standing on the grass screaming. One of the workers picked her up and quickly realised she had stinging ants all over her legs. The worker brushed the ants off and handed the girl to Laura, to be bathed. The little girl didn't seem to know what was happening as Laura soaped and bathed her, but by the end of the evening she gave Laura a big smile. Without any words, Laura showed the love that Jesus has for this child.

Many children have been touched by God's love in this way. Sarapeen had already had a rough life by the age of six. Things started to go wrong when both her parents died. Her grandmother took her in. But instead of caring for the girl, she sent Sarapeen every week to a town near the border with Thailand, in order to beg for money. With no other family to turn to, Sarapeen did as she was told. During the week she lived on the streets, returning on weekends to bring her earnings to her grandmother.

When the Hischild workers found Sarapeen, she was very weak and covered from head to toe with an itchy skin infection called scabies. They took her to the Hischild orphanage south of Phnom Penh, where she was cleaned up and given medical treatment. Now Sarapeen has a new family: fifty boys and girls have been rescued and live at the orphanage. There they hear about God's love. They see it in action every day in the kindness and care they receive.

Lots of groups are trying to help the children of Cambodia. Yet there are still children digging in the rubbish heaps or working in 'sweatshops'. These are factories crammed full of children as young as seven. They work from early morning until late evening, operating machines to stitch clothing, then go to sleep in the same room where they work. The next morning they get up and start all over again.

I imagine that your life is very different from these children. You probably go to a good school, have plenty to eat and don't have to work for your living. What can you do, to help the children of Cambodia? For now, you might check with international groups such as World Vision, Tearfund or Samaritan's Purse, to see if they have a project that helps children like this. You could encourage your family or church to help support one of these projects, or to sponsor a child.

Finally, pray about what God has for you in the future. When you grow up, you could help make a difference as a teacher or mission worker in a country like Cambodia.

Jesus taught his followers to pray, 'Father, may your name be honoured. May your Kingdom come soon.' (Luke 11:2) You don't have to go to a foreign country, to be part of building up God's kingdom here on earth. Even now, no matter how young you are, God wants you to live in such a way that people will sense his love and be drawn to him.

Jesus said, 'Let the children come to me. Don't stop them! For the Kingdom of God belongs to such as these. I assure you, anyone who doesn't have their kind of faith will never get into the Kingdom of God.' (Mark 10: 14-15)

The Lost Generation

Chea waves goodbye to his mother and unlocks his bicycle from the shed in front of their house. He pedals quickly down the rutted unpaved street. His friend Thon lives nearby, and most days they bike together to school.

The rising sun is just touching the rooftops of the city of Phnom Penh. Chea hears cocks crowing, and the chanting of monks as he cycles past the Buddhist temple. He feels confused. Last night his father told him again the story of how, when his father was a boy, he and his family had to flee the city and work as peasants on a farm, to escape being killed by soldiers. Often they had only one small pot of rice each day to share with ten people.

This is a story he has heard many times from his father, and he's always believed it. It is a terrible tale. His father's parents and several other family members were killed by a group known as the Khmer Rouge, or 'red Cambodians'. Other family members starved to death. But yesterday his friend Thon told him, 'My parents say the stories of all those killings are not true. And even if they are partly true, we should forget about them. Cambodia should forget the past and look to the future.'

Chea turns his friend's words over and over in his mind. He doesn't want to disagree with Thon, but he knows his father would never make something like this up. And anyway, if it didn't happen, where are his father's parents? Where are the rest of his father's family?

It is hard to believe something so awful could happen, but it did. During a time of turmoil in Cambodia, the Khmer Rouge forced everyone to leave the cities and work as farm labourers in the villages. They insisted people all dress alike in black jackets and trousers which looked like pyjamas. Everyone had the same hair style. No one was allowed to practice any kind of religion. People were forbidden from using certain words, like 'mama' or 'daddy' – all people were meant to be exactly the same. If you called your mother 'mama' that would show respect to her and it would set her apart, which the Khmer Rouge said was wrong.

A country where everyone looks alike and no one is allowed to respect another person sounds very dreary. But the worst thing the Khmer Rouge did was to execute many of their own countrymen, people whose only 'crime' was to be doctors or teachers or educated people. Even people who wore glasses were killed, because they were suspected of being intelligent. For four years, from 1975 to 1979, nearly two million Cambodians were murdered or starved to death.

Many people were taken to a school in Phnom Penh which was turned into a prison and place of torture. About 14,000 people went through the Toul Sleng prison. Those who did not die there were taken to an area outside Phnom Penh and killed. That place is now called the Killing Fields.

A man named Comrade Duch (pronounced 'Doik') was the director of the prison. He gave orders for things which are too awful to write in this book. Do you ever wonder what will happen to a person like that after he dies? Will God punish him for his horrible crimes?

We might say 'Yes, of course!' But God had other plans. Later, Duch repented of his crimes. He came to understand that Jesus had died even for the torture that Duch had caused. This evil general put his trust in Jesus and gave his life to follow him. As I write this, he is in prison awaiting trial. He will have to pay for his crimes. But if he has sincerely trusted in Jesus, God sees him as a forgiven child and will welcome him into heaven. If God can forgive the sin of the director of Toul Sleng prison, he can forgive anyone!

It's important to remember as well, that although horrible things happen in the world, that's not the whole story. One day God will bring all suffering to an end. He will reign over a new heaven and new earth, where there will be no death or crying or pain. He will live right among us, and wipe every tear from our eyes. (Revelation 21: 1-4)

Until that time, there are things we can do, to help make peace on earth. Not long ago, former prisoners of Toul Sleng were brought to meet their former prison guards, the very people who had beaten and tortured them. Together they visited the prison and the mass graves of the Killing Fields. Each side spoke of what they experienced. The guards apologised, saying they were under orders and had acted to save their lives. Not all of the prisoners were able to forgive their former captors, but some did.

How about you? You may have done something that you knew was wrong, which hurt another person. Did you go to that person and say you were sorry? Did you mean it? Or perhaps you got angry over something done to you. Have you forgiven the other person – even if they haven't asked you to? If we hold anger in our heart, it grows and puts down roots. Then it turns into a nasty thing called bitterness. We become bitter when we are angry over something for a long time. Bitterness is very hard to get rid of, and it takes up lots of space in our hearts – space that God wants to fill with good things. If you have trouble saying sorry or forgiving, ask God to help you with this.

If you walk the streets of towns and cities in Cambodia today, you don't see many elderly people. Over half of the population are under the age of 25. These young people have no first-hand knowledge of what life was like under the Khmer Rouge. The older generation who lived through the terror may want to forget about it and move on, but something so dreadful can't be tucked away in a secret place. It has to be brought into the open so that the country can be healed.

Dave and Laura's friend, Jun, grew up during the years of civil war that followed the Khmer Rouge reign. 'One of my earliest memories was listening to the sound of heavy gunfire while trying to sleep,' Jun says. In the daytime, his mother would send him and his older brother into the woods to avoid being caught by government soldiers, who wanted to take young boys to fight against the Khmer Rouge.

'We used to hide in the woods and play all day. We were not allowed to come back to the house until night. That way, when the soldiers came to our house, my mother could say: "I have no children here to fight in your war."'

Even worse than the government soldiers were the Khmer Rouge soldiers who were hiding in the jungles. They were desperate for ammunition, food, medical supplies and anything they could sell or barter. These soldiers would attack villages at night, taking what they wanted and killing anyone who got in their way.

Often when Jun and his mother and brothers were asleep on the floor of their house, they would hear shouts and gunfire. Jun would be wide awake in an instant! Imagine the scene: they dart down the ladder to the ground and dive into a small underground shelter. Jun's mother pulls branches of wood and palm leaves over the top, and the three crouch there, trying not to cough or breathe too loudly. They hear laughing and clanking as the soldiers rummage through their house. These men will steal their cooking pot and the car battery that provides their electricity. But Jun's mother doesn't care. At least her family is safe.

Jun's father had died from malaria when Jun was only two years old. It was up to his mother to protect her three boys through the daily dangers of war. However, she could only keep Jun safe when he was at home. At school there were other dangers. One thing made Jun stand out: he was the only Christian in the school.

At first, the other children simply asked him why he wasn't a Buddhist like everyone else. Before long, they began to tease him openly and sometimes spat at him. One day a group of his classmates decided to have some fun. They bound Jun's wrists together and dragged him out of the school gate and down the village street. They ripped his only school shirt to pieces and scratched him with their fingernails.

But this persecution only made his faith stronger. He decided from a young age that he was going to follow God. He was determined not to be put off by people taunting or hurting him. When his classmates saw that the teasing didn't work, they stopped doing it and Jun began to make friends.

When he was eighteen, Jun moved to Phnom Penh to attend Bible college, before going on to work for a Christian development agency known as *Asian Outreach Cambodia*. He now gives health education to poor children and young people who live on the Mekong River flood plain.

Jun is known by his friends as a loyal, fun-loving person. He has suffered much hardship at the hands of others, but he has learned the art of forgiveness and *reconciliation*. While forgiveness means saying sorry to each other and not holding a grudge, reconciliation goes further than that. It means bringing together people who once had a relationship, and healing the past wounds so that they can have a relationship again in the future.

It is almost thirty years since the end of the Khmer Rouge reign of terror. Soon trials will begin, for the criminals who ordered the torture and murder of thousands of Khmer. It not yet clear what the outcome will be, but many people hope for reconciliation.

Think about someone you have forgiven. Have you also been reconciled to that person? Are you friends again, or do you still avoid spending time with each other? What does God want you to do about this? He will show you if you ask him to.

In some ways, Cambodia is a country which has been erased, rubbed out. It had to start over almost from scratch. After the time of the Khmer Rouge, the country was closed to outsiders. It was only in 1991 that development agencies were allowed in, to help rebuild this shattered nation.

Pray for this country full of young people, that many of them like Jun will put their lives and their futures into the hands of our faithful God. Pray that those involved in the Khmer Rouge will be deeply sorry for their crimes and find forgiveness in coming to know Jesus. Ask God to help people on both sides to be reconciled, in order to build this country again.

Do not repay evil with evil or insult with insult, but with blessing, because to this you were called, so that you may inherit a blessing. (1 Peter 3.9)

How to Have Fun in Cambodia

How do you like to have fun? Do you love sports like swimming or playing football or other games? Do you enjoy reading? Or maybe your favourite thing is playing games on a screen.

Football (soccer) is popular with kids in Cambodia, just as in the UK. However, there is a difference. Instead of playing on grass, Cambodian children play football in the unpaved streets or on any patch of waste ground – usually barefoot! Dave enjoys joining in what might be called 'bare-footie' with kids living on his street, or youth from the Young Life club. He was excited to be asked to attend a Premier League match at the city stadium.

He thought the stadium would be packed, to see the Phnom Penh team play. But it was almost empty. Another surprise was the style of play which was completely crazy, with everyone on attack and no one on defense. All the players were just running from end to end on the pitch.

Then things got even worse. The visiting team wasn't happy with a referee call against them, so they decided to injure someone from the Phnom Penh side. They threw one of the players to the ground with a two-footed tackle, and suddenly all the players and coaches from both teams rushed onto the pitch and started shoving each other. Then someone landed a kung-fu kick at the referee! Finally the military police ran out with guns, trying to restore order. This was the final straw for the visiting team, who took off their shirts, threw them on the ground in disgust and marched off. Phnom Penh 'won' the match by default.

So, if you enjoy football, you might be able to watch it in Cambodia, if you can put up with chaos on the pitch, or play it if you don't mind going barefoot. But if you like to read books, you might find it hard. Children's books are not widely available, and most village schools don't even have a library. The pupils get to read only the books that are provided in the classroom.

If you like to play games on a screen, there again you won't get much chance, unless your family is wealthy. Most homes do not have computers or television games.

What do kids do for fun? Well, they play simple games outdoors, such as *leak kanseng* or 'scarf hiding'. This is somewhat like 'duck, duck, goose' or 'drop the hankie'. Children sit in a circle, while one child runs around the circle behind them, holding a knotted *krama* or scarf. The runner drops the scarf behind one person, who then jumps up and chases the runner, trying to hit them with the scarf. In another game, two children dig ten holes in the ground. They have 42 stones which they place in the holes and remove according to a system. When all the holes are empty, the person who has the highest number of stones wins. In the game *vay kaorm* one person is blindfolded and given a stick, with which he tries to hit a clay pot until it breaks.

Tug-of-war is a popular sport, as is wrestling. Before a wrestling match, the combatants perform a ritual dance to the beat of drums. All these games and sports are especially popular during the Cambodian New Year celebrations, which last for several days in the spring.

One of the most common activities in Cambodia, which occurs all year round, is betting. Even young children playing football in the street will place bets of a few pennies on who will score first in their game. If you don't want to bet, they won't play with you. At the corner of every major road in Phnom Penh is a tiny betting stall, often run by someone who also sells vegetables or cooked food. Kids grow up with the idea that betting and gambling are a normal part of life.

During the last World Cup, Cambodians gambled huge amounts of money, placing bets on which teams they thought would win in each match. They bet not only money but cows, motorcycles or even their houses. They thought they might make a big win and stop being so poor. Unfortunately most of them lost, and were much worse off than before. The government has tried to stop this kind of gambling, but it still goes on.

Along with gambling, many people in Cambodia ask advice from fortune tellers, thinking this will make them happy. They want to find out what the future holds, or to get help making a decision. Should they buy a certain house? What about that young man their daughter likes? Is he the right husband for her? Cambodians may pay as much as a month's wages to ask a fortune teller questions like this.

They think if they can find out what will happen in the future, they can keep bad things from happening. But only God knows the future, and only he has the power to lead us through life in the right way. He will guide us if we ask him to, and without charging anything!

People who gamble or go to fortune tellers are showing that they don't really understand what God is like. Maybe they think he isn't big enough or strong enough to help them. Or they don't believe he loves them and wants what is best for them. We can't see God, so it is easy to get confused about what he is like. That's one reason he sent Jesus, so we could see God in action. If you want to know more about what Jesus is like, why not read one of the books of the Bible such as Mark or Luke which tell the story of his life on earth.

Another fun thing to do in Cambodia is attend a wedding. If you are there during wedding season, which takes place in the dry months of November to April, you can hardly avoid being part of one. You may be walking down a side street in Phnom Penh when suddenly you come upon a huge silk canopy which completely blocks the road from side to side. Loud wailing music fills the air, and through the open front of the canopy you glimpse young women in beautiful long silk gowns. You see young men wearing crisp white shirts, black trousers and shiny black shoes.

There are no pavements, so you have no way to get around the wedding. The only way is to go right through the middle of it. When this happened to us, Dave urged us to walk quickly. He said the bride and groom would love to have foreigners in their wedding pictures. As weddings last up to three days, we could be there a long time!

On the first day of a wedding, just after dawn, the groom and his family arrive at the bride's house bringing meats, fruits, pastries and a cooked pig's head. Everyone on the street knows they are there, from the loud noise of traditional instruments such as drums, bamboo flutes and special fiddles made of coconut shell. Then the bride and groom and all the relatives may parade through the streets to the site of the wedding, banging pots and chanting. Sometimes people throw flower petals from their balconies as the procession passes by.

Dave and Laura were invited to the wedding of their neighbour, Sambat. They were surprised that Sambat changed her dress several times during the day of symbolic ritual. A bride will typically wear up to fifteen different outfits during her wedding. Sambat asked Laura to lead her into the ceremonial room and present her to the groom for the foot-washing ceremony. It was quite an honour, and Laura felt nervous as the eyes of all the wedding guests were on her.

In the old days, for the foot-washing the bride would place the groom's feet on a tray and wash them. However today the bride sprays cologne on his feet. The wedding ends with a knot-tying ceremony in which close family and friends are invited to tie ribbons around the wrists of the bride and also the groom. This is a way to wish blessings on the couple and they will each wear them for three days afterwards.

If you are invited to lots of weddings in Cambodia, as many young people are, this can be a problem because you are expected to bring money. When guests arrive, they put some money in a bowl. A family member will record the guest's name and the amount given. This helps pay for the wedding, yet it is hard in a country where the average salary is only a few pounds a day. If you are a foreigner, you are expected to give more than the other guests.

Cambodians like having fun, whether it's playing games or going to weddings. But there is a darker side to life here. The people live with the danger of diseases such as malaria or dengue fever, or traffic accidents which are the main cause of death.

Imagine that you are in a traffic accident. You need to be taken to hospital, quickly! Your family brings you to the hospital, where they are told, 'No money, no treatment!' They must pay to get you seen by a doctor. So they pay, and you are put into a hospital bed. It is a metal frame with no mattress, in a room with many other patients. There are no screens on the windows, no sheets on the bed, no towels for you to use, no water to drink, no food to eat.

The doctor comes and examines you. He says you need medicine and an X-ray. 'Do you have money to pay for these?' he asks. Again your family hears the depressing words, 'No money, no treatment!'

The doctor is supposed to treat the patients without charging, so he is in effect asking for a bribe. Yet doctors' salaries are very low. Without this extra money he would not be able to keep working.

Your family brings in netting to protect you from malaria-causing mosquitoes, a straw mat for your mattress, towels, drinking water and food which they will cook over a fire built on the floor of the hospital ward. They will take it in turns to be with you day and night, as there are no nurses on this ward. Families are expected to care for the patients themselves. They bring mats to lay on the dirty floor; that is where they will sleep. Meanwhile they try and think where they can get some money to pay for the expensive tests and medicines you desperately need.

Dave and Laura's friend, Dina, was knocked off her bike and taken to hospital. When they visited her they were shocked to find blood stains on the walls, used bandages on the floor and the whole place stinking. Dina's friends were able to pay for painkillers and a scan, and she has recovered well. Yet still the problem of health care in Cambodia continues.

Whether we live in a poor or wealthy country, life isn't always fun. We don't know what's around the corner. Jesus said that we would have troubles on earth. Yet he asks his followers to find peace in him. Jesus does not take away all our problems, but he does give us his love and wisdom so that we can go through them in a better way. We can be encouraged because a special friend walks with us in the midst of our problems. We all need friends, but especially Jesus, the most faithful and true friend we could ever have.

Jesus said, 'I have told you all this so that you may have peace in me. Here on earth you will have many trials and sorrows. But take heart, because I have overcome the world.' (John 16:33)

The Most Special Birthday

Do you know when your birthday is? Of course you do! But you might not, if you live in Cambodia. Generally, birthdays are not celebrated until after a person turns fifty. Older people are treated with respect, and families honour their older members with a birthday feast to celebrate their long lives, but not the younger ones.

That sounds harsh. You may be thinking, those poor Cambodian children! They never have the excitement of looking forward to that one day in the year which is their very own special day.

Yet it is not quite that bad. Children do celebrate being a year older at Cambodian New Year, which falls in April in our calendar. Everyone born before April becomes one year older at that time. This can be confusing: for example, if you are born in March, you become one year old in April, when your actual age would be one month old.

Even so, age is important because there are different titles for you according to your age and the age of the person you are speaking with. You might be asked when you first meet someone how old you are. Two young people will speak to each other using different words from a young person talking with an older person.

Turning a year older is just one thing that makes New Year the most exciting holiday in Cambodia. The hard work of harvesting rice is finished. It's a time to celebrate and forget all the troubles of the past year, before the rainy season starts.

Kids throng the streets during the several days of the New Year festival, trying to see if they can throw water or talcum powder – or a combination of both – onto their unsuspecting friends. Perhaps it's the Cambodian version of snowball fights! They will also try and dump powder on people who are riding by on motos. When they see foreigners they may be a bit hesitant – will these westerners mind being doused with white powder? But often the bold ones will go ahead and throw it.

All ages get together and play games in the street during New Year. Normally older boys and girls play separately, but New Year is different. In a popular game using giant flat conkers (chestnuts) called *ankun*, teams of boys and girls compete to see who can knock down the other team's standing conkers. If one team wins, they are allowed to rap two conkers on the knees of the other team. This doesn't hurt but makes a very loud noise.

People give their houses a thorough cleaning at this season. They believe this will get rid of any evil spirits inside the house. They also make new clothes to represent a fresh start.

The Bible also uses the idea of clothing to indicate a fresh start. The mention of white clothing in the Bible often refers to a person having a clean and pure heart before God. If you have trusted in Jesus to save you, you are clean in God's eyes. He has forgiven you completely. You belong to him, and you will go to heaven and be with him when you die. But becoming a Christian doesn't make you perfect. You will still sometimes do or think things that don't please God.

How do you keep your heart pure? Most important of all, obey God's Word (Psalm 119:9). The moment you notice you have done something wrong, tell God you are sorry. You can do this silently, in your heart. Don't save it all up to the end of the day – you'll probably forget about it by then. Just ask God to forgive you, and thank him that he already has. If you have hurt someone else, you may need to go to them and apologise. When you sincerely ask God's forgiveness, you can count on him to give it. He won't keep bringing up what you did or nag you about it. You will be at peace with him.

Buddhists seek to make peace with their spirits at New Year. Most people leave the city and travel back to the province in the countryside where their family comes from. There they will visit the local Buddhist temple during the day, offering gifts to the spirits of their dead ancestors. They believe if they don't do this, the ancestors will be angry and do them harm. They also help build a small 'mountain' out of sand on the temple grounds. Each grain of sand is thought to add more health and happiness to a person's life.

Cambodian Christians also celebrate New Year, but with a difference. For example, during the festival Jun and his brothers show honour and respect to their mother, who is living, but not to their father who died many years ago. They don't go to the temple during the day to make offerings to the dead.

They know that their father who died is in heaven, and he does not need offerings to keep him from getting angry at them.

Being a follower of Jesus is not like being Buddhist or following any other religion. Christians don't need to give Jesus extra gifts to try and make him happy. They know they already have peace with God through what Jesus did on the cross. It isn't a matter of trying hard to follow lots of rules. They can trust in what God has already done for them, and thank him for it.

At night during New Year, the local temple area becomes a place for all the community to get together in a carnival atmosphere. Christian families will join in these activities and have fun with their relatives and friends. At New Year everyone becomes a year older and gifts are given, but more often it's children giving their parents, aunts and uncles gifts, to show them respect.

Showing respect to our parents is a good idea, at any time of year. We may not always like what our parents do, but they still deserve our esteem because God has put them in charge of us while we are young. He wants us to thank him for them and show them regard. Have you thanked your parents recently for all they do for you? Try it – you may get a surprised look!

Although birthdays are not celebrated in Cambodia, there is one very special baby whose birthday is observed: Jesus! We arrived in Cambodia on Christmas eve. In this Buddhist country, we did not expect to spot any signs of Christmas. How surprised we were to see Christmas lights and decorations in the shops, and even plastic Christmas trees and cards with Santa's face! Stores advertise 'Christmas Sales'. Flashing lights and large Christmas decorations hang in the gardens and villas of well-to-do Khmer. But something is missing.

Do Cambodians know they are celebrating the birth of Jesus? Not really. They view it as a way to sell goods and make more money. Christmas day is a normal business day in the city. People go 'Christmas shopping' and some even give presents, but most don't know it has anything to do with the birth of Jesus Christ.

Dave and Laura asked their neighbours what they thought Christmas was all about. 'We don't know,' they replied. 'But even you foreigners need to celebrate something. We have our Water Festival and you have your Christmas.'

A Phnom Penh newspaper interviewed workers in shops which were decorated for Christmas, asking what they thought Christmas meant. 'I have no idea,' said one employee, while another chimed in, 'But we love Christmas. It's so cool. I want to play in the snow one day too.' A store manager said, 'Christmas is about a big fat guy giving presents to small kids.' Eventually the reporter found someone who said, 'I think Christmas has something to do with Jesus Christ. Maybe it's his birthday? I'm just guessing.'

Even though Cambodians don't know much about it, they see Christmas as a fun Western thing to celebrate. So churches and Christian groups use the season as a time to tell people about Jesus.

They may hire a large venue and invite lots of people to come to a Christmas party. It's a chance for people to have a good time and learn about Christmas customs, but also to hear the real story behind the celebration.

In Phnom Penh we attended the Young Life Christmas party, where around seventy-five teenagers gathered to learn about Christmas. We were greeted by a bearded Santa Claus, sweating in his red suit in the thirty-five degree heat. He handed us packs of mango-flavoured chewing gum from his sack, and we kicked off our sandals and joined everyone seated on the floor inside the small hall. After some games my husband Roger gave a talk on the real meaning of Christmas. Most of these Khmer teens listened intently to the story of why Jesus came to earth.

It's a challenge to explain the true meaning of Christmas in a strongly Buddhist country like Cambodia, where people know very little about Jesus, the Bible or the Christian faith. During the Christmas season, Dave and Laura decided to show God's love in practical ways to their Cambodian friends. They helped throw a party for street children, and also gave little 'goodie bags' to their neighbours.

You are probably expecting some nice presents for Christmas, and also thinking about what you can give your family members. I hope your family also takes time at Christmas to think about the real reason for the giving — that God came down to us as a human, someone we could understand and relate to.

But have you thought about giving to people who don't know you, who can never come back and thank you? As you walk down any city street in Cambodia, you see lots of poor and needy people. You may not see beggars or orphans where you live, but needy people do exist. Perhaps you and your family could plan this year to celebrate Christmas with a difference.

Charities such as Samaritan's Purse, Traidcraft, World Vision and many others, offer ways you can buy a Christmas present for someone in a *developing country*. This means a poor country which is trying to improve life for its people. You might give money to help build a water well, or buy a goat or a wheelchair for someone on the other side of the globe. Your dad may not need any more ties. Perhaps he'd rather know that a family in Africa got some baby chicks!

In the Book of Matthew, Jesus explains to his disciples that 'whatever you did for one of the least of these, you did for me' and 'whatever you did not do for one of the least of these, you did not do for me'. So, when you give to people like this, you're really giving to God. Also, these organisations have ongoing relationships with poor countries. They're not simply giving material items. They also tell people how to know Jesus and how to grow in him.

Here's a wild idea: some families use the time off at Christmas or during the summer to travel to another county and do short-term missions. They may help build a well, paint a church building, help with English or teach people about Jesus. The website www.christianvocations.org could give you some ideas.

You might also decide as a family to give some time to the 'least of these' in your local community this Christmas. Whether at a church, homeless project or shelter, there is bound to be an opportunity to volunteer your time. I imagine you will enjoy Christmas even more than when you merely stay at home and get presents and eat to bursting.

The Christmas sales and gaudy decorations in Cambodia mean very little. But God is working behind the scenes. All over the country there are small groups of people who are followers of Jesus. They know that Christmas celebrates the time when God came down from heaven to earth, and they want their friends and neighbours to know it too. These Christians pray it will only be a matter of time until more and more Cambodians start asking, 'What is Christmas all about?'

So the Word became human and lived here on earth among us. He was full of unfailing love and faithfulness. And we have seen his glory, the glory of the only Son of the Father. (John 1:14)

Tigers, Mine Dogs and the Word of God

You are strapped into your seat in a Cessna aeroplane on your way north from Phnom Penh to the far borders of Cambodia. The roar of the engine is deafening – no chance to talk to your companions, so you look out the window. The small plane flies below the clouds. You see three mighty rivers merging below you, then endless rice fields covered in a blanket of water, the result of months of rain. After the rice paddies come rubber tree plantations, followed by hills shrouded in thick forest.

The outer provinces of Cambodia have a character all of their own. In the western provinces you will encounter a unique dog who has a highly dangerous job. In the northeast, you will find waterfalls and groups of people who speak separate languages.

Imagine your plane has landed in western Battambang province, which borders Thailand. You are coming to join a group of people who are walking in the countryside. But this is no ordinary rambling club. Everyone is wearing special helmets and body protectors. Several carry metal detectors. One of them has a dog on a lead.

The highly skilled Alsatian (German Shepherd) strains at the lead as it sniffs the earth. Suddenly it lies down on the ground, which signals the handler that it's found something. What has the dog spotted, and why is the handler wearing a helmet and protective vest?

This is a Mine Detection Dog or MDD, which is trained to sniff out landmines and unexploded devices which lie under the surface of the ground. During the years of war with the Khmer Rouge, many landmines were buried and many bombs were dropped on Cambodia. These dangerous weapons lie invisible under the soil, waiting until someone innocently steps on them to explode. Some of them are not much larger than an ordinary bath plug. A farmer could be ploughing up the land behind a team of oxen, getting ready to plant a crop, and step on a landmine. Or perhaps some children are playing a game outside, and one of them finds a metal object under the dirt. It looks like a bowling pin, so they decide to set it up and throw rocks at it. But it's an unexploded weapon.

Although the Khmer Rouge wars ended many years ago, millions of landmines are still hiding in the ground, mostly in the northwest provinces. It's very easy to stick a landmine in the dirt, but finding them and disarming them is difficult and expensive. Many charities have been working hard for years to clear the land and make it usable again. Every square metre of suspect land has to be checked. That's where the dogs come in.

You may be worried that the dogs are in danger. However, their incredibly keen sense of smell makes them safe. A dog's nose is so sensitive, it can sniff out one drop of blood in a bucket full of water! They are taught to react even to a small concentration of TNT, a chemical found in landmines and weapons. The dogs will lie down the instant they sense an explosive. It takes about

two years to train a puppy to be a landmine dog, using techniques similar to those for dogs who sniff out drugs.

The mine clearers often use metal detectors instead of dogs to find hidden landmines. But the metal detector will signal any kind of metal in the ground. The trained dogs, on the other hand, won't be confused by tin cans or any other metal. They will only point out explosives. They can detect a weapon even if it is made of plastic or buried deep beneath the surface. Their main job is to help the mine clearers know which area is scattered with mines or weapons.

Once the landmine team know where the mines are, they have to explode them. This is often done using a specially designed mechanical brush cutter, a large vehicle which looks like a cross between a tank and a digger. It clears the land and sets off any explosives lurking underneath the soil.

You may be very glad that you don't face dangers of landmines every day. But sometimes belonging to God's kingdom can feel dangerous. You may be the only Christian in your family, which can be very hard. Or perhaps kids at school make fun of you. It isn't easy to stand up for what you believe, when others don't see it that way. When Jesus lived on earth, he faced these kinds of problems every day, so he understands exactly what you have to go through. Whatever the challenges, they are worth it. Nothing on earth compares with the value of knowing Jesus and being able to live as his friend every day.

Although the mine dogs do their job well, they do have one problem: they come from cooler countries and are not used to the intense Cambodian heat. So their handlers set up umbrellas for the dogs to rest under during the day, and put fans in their kennels at night. Their handlers have a close relationship with them. The life of a mine dog is very different to that of most Cambodian dogs, which are kept as guard dogs and not treated as pets. Their owners may not even bother to feed them! Most dogs in this country have to forage for whatever scraps they can find.

Let's travel now to the eastern provinces of Rattanakiri and Mondulkiri, which border Laos and Vietnam. Most of the people living in these areas are not Khmer at all, but instead belong to one of several minority groups. Each has its own language and customs. Many of the people do not speak the Khmer language, so they are cut off from what goes on in the rest of the country. Religion is important to their daily lives. Some believe in gods of nature and the spirits that they think live in the forest. The people are careful to do whatever they can to try and keep these gods happy.

When Dave and Laura visited Rattanakiri, they travelled to a village where the Tampuan people lived. They were driven in a

4x4 which slogged through deep mud, sometimes almost toppling over. After a couple of hours of being thrown around in the back seat, they arrived at a village of small houses made from palm leaves. All around was lush jungle.

Unlike most Khmer people, the Tampuan are shy. Children peered around doors and through windows to stare at the white strangers, but they didn't dare come out. One special feature of the village was the community shower. The villagers had built a channel from bamboo shoots. This bamboo pipeline brings water from a spring high in the mountains and carries it down to their valley. Every day the people have to walk all the way down a steep hill to get water and shower.

Laura watched as one woman, still fully clothed, stood under the running water and scrubbed herself all over with a small stick. She also filled her water container, which was the shell of a large dried fruit. Imagine having to hike to a place outside your town, every time you wanted to get some water or have a wash. Once you get there, you take a shower with all your clothes on! Then you have to hike back up the hill, carrying the water you need for that day.

Many people here do not read or write any language, even their own. In some cases, their languages have not been written down. The community has passed down the language from generation to generation only by speaking. So someone has to first decide how to write the language, then teach the people to read it.

This is the kind of work done in many parts of the world by Bible translators. A translation team will settle in an area, get to know the people, their customs, and their language. They will begin writing down the people's speech using phonetic symbols. Then they teach the people to read their own language.

Not only that, but they begin to translate books of the Bible, so the community can hear God speaking to them in their everyday speech. Throughout the world there are nearly 3000 minority groups which do not have any of the Bible in their own language.

People like the Tampuan are also being taught to read and speak the national Khmer language, so they will be able to communicate and deal with the world beyond their small group. In the Tampuan village, Dave and Laura sat in on a class of village women who were learning their numbers. They also met local volunteer teachers who are trained to teach their own language as well as Khmer.

There are many exotic animals which thrive in the tropical climate of the provinces. But there is one animal you probably won't see: the Indochinese tiger. Tigers roam through a large area at night, seeking whatever animals they can find for food. These powerful animals have been known to terrorize whole villages, killing the water buffalo which the farmers need to work the land.

However, there's not much danger of running into one, although you might hear its hoarse cry from a distance. They live deep in the forests on the borders of Cambodia, and their numbers are shrinking. A dead tiger can be sold to make traditional

Chinese medicine, so poor people may see them as a way to make money. Also, during the years of warfare large areas of forest were destroyed by chemicals, and still other areas are being cleared for development. The tiger's habitat is getting smaller all the time, and the animals they feed on are disappearing as well. The Indochinese tiger is considered 'critically endangered' by the World Wildlife Federation. Only about a thousand are left in Southeast Asia. They may soon become extinct if nothing is done.

When you visit a zoo and see the tigers, you may feel sorry for these grand animals who are cooped up in an enclosure. But zoos around the world help keep various endangered species of tiger alive. They often trade tigers with each other, so that they can have a pair of tigers which are most likely to produce healthy cubs. By the way, did you know that each tiger's stripes are unique? They are like our fingerprints. Look out for this next time you see two tigers at the zoo.

Laura had an unexpected encounter with a tropical creature in Rattanakiri. She and Dave were eating at a typical restaurant, an open area covered with a wooden roof. Laura happened to be sitting next to one of the poles which held up the roof. She was calmly eating her dinner when all of a sudden she felt something touch her head. She turned her head and came face-to-face with a large gecko! It had crawled down the pole and onto her shoulder. She yelped and the gecko leaped onto the tile floor and scurried away.

If you travel to anywhere in Cambodia, you will very likely see a gecko, or at least hear them squawking in the roof at night. These are speckled lizards that can grow up to 35 centimetres long. Don't try to pick one up – they can bite humans, although they are usually just glad to get out of your way. These acrobatic creatures can climb up a glass window and hang from the ceiling by one foot. Don't try this yourself, unless you have very hairy feet! That's the gecko's secret: each of its feet is covered with half a million tiny hairs with split ends. These allow them to stick firmly to any surface, even under water! Scientists have been studying the gecko's foot hair and also the way its toes curl backwards, to help improve the way robots move over rough ground.

In Rattanakiri you are likely to see elephants and even be offered a ride on one. You climb up some stairs attached to the outside of a house, and the handler leads his elephant over until its head is right next to you. You step onto the animal's wrinkled forehead, then clamber up onto a small platform strapped to its back. The handler takes his place astride the elephant's neck, and off you go!

At first you feel seasick, as you sway back and forth with the

mammoth creature's stride, but eventually you get used to it. It's a leisurely way to see the countryside, especially if your elephant decides to stop every so often and munch grass, which he plucks with his trunk. From your high vantage point you enjoy the view of a rubber tree plantation and then waterfalls in the jungle. Finally you reach your destination, a clear calm lake which was formed in an extinct volcano. It feels like you are on another planet, millions of miles away from the hubbub of the city.

All too soon, it's time to leave the provinces and head back to crowded, crazy Phnom Penh. As your tiny plane flies over the jungle, then the rice fields and finally the place where the three great rivers meet, you think about what God must see when he looks at Cambodia. He sees people living in poverty, barely scraping a living from the land, and fearful of the spirits they believe in. He sees people injured by landmines, and others hurt by cruelty and greed. But also, he sees people reaching out to those in need, bringing hope through God's Word. He sees those who have received the gift of new life which Jesus offers. They know they don't have to fear the old gods, because they have found the one true God, and he loves them very much.

For the Word of God is full of living power. It is sharper than the sharpest knife, cutting deep into our inmost thoughts and desires. (Hebrews 4:12)

From Useless to Useful

'Ay-jay! Ay-jay!' The boy walks down the dusty Phnom Penh street, pulling a wooden cart piled with rubbish sacks. 'Ay-jay!' he calls loudly.

A woman comes out of her house and waves for him to stop. She hands him a sack filled with discarded plastic bottles and tin cans. The boy tosses her sack onto his cart. He will sell all these things to recyclers and be able to buy food for that day. Used bottles and cans might seem worthless to us, but to this boy they are treasure.

Surprising things can become valuable in Cambodia. Tourists in the country are often impressed by the many beautiful handicrafts for sale. Some of these are made from objects that were discarded, thrown away by someone who thought they had no use. For example, a coconut shell can be turned into a lovely bowl; a large sack used to carry fish food can be made into a sturdy and attractive handbag. Old magazines are cut, rolled and glued into beads for necklaces! Water buffalo horns are turned into ornaments and spoons, and plastic water bottles are re-used for any kind of liquid, from oil to soya milk to petrol.

Many Cambodians earn their living by making crafts out of rubbish that would have been thrown away. Some of these workers are people who might have felt discarded themselves, because they are disabled. But they have learned how to make something useful and are able to support their families.

Textiles made of silk are some of the most beautiful handiwork from Cambodia. In many villages you see women sitting on the platforms underneath their houses, weaving silk on wooden looms. This cloth may eventually be made into an expensive dress or handbag and be sold at a boutique in a city like Paris. Yet it came from a poor village, woven by a woman who may not have much training and may get paid very little for her work.

Before it can be woven, though, the silk must be produced by women who practise the ancient art of *sericulture*. This is the process of growing silkworms and extracting the silk. The skill of sericulture has been handed down from mother to daughter through the generations and still thrives.

The silkworm breeder must first plant mulberry trees, as the worms will only eat leaves from this tree. The silk butterfly lays its tiny eggs on the mulberry leaves and then dies. The breeder incubates the eggs, protecting them under a loose cover and a piece of wet cloth until they hatch into worms called *larvae*. The worms are placed on a platform of freshly picked and chopped mulberry leaves. The breeder has to bring fresh leaves several times a day for the hungry silkworms. She must also shield the platform from heat and smoke and from other insects which would eat the worms.

When the worms are ready to spin silk, they raise their heads and begin to rock back and forth. This is a sign they are producing

the thin strands of silk from their digestive glands, and are starting to wrap them around their bodies. At that point the breeder places the worms on bundles of twigs where they stay for three or four days, until they have wound themselves with about 30 layers of golden silk yarn. The breeder then has the delicate task of unwinding the thin strands from the worm without breaking them. Finally she cleans them and spins them into thread.

As for the poor worm, it will probably end up sold for food. They are said to be delicious fried with garlic! It's another example of something that might be thrown away being used to a good purpose.

Now the silk yarn will be hand-dyed, either using chemicals or natural dyes from leaves, wood, bark or flowers. Then it will be spun by hand onto large bobbins, ready for weaving. It takes up to 100 silkworm cocoons to produce one bobbin of yarn.

The next step is weaving. You need a lot of patience for this job: two people spend about three days preparing a large wooden

loom with thread. Weaving by hand in the traditional way, a worker can produce only about two metres of cloth per day. Electric looms produce about five metres per day. The cloth is then sewn into bedspreads, scarves, wall hangings, pillowcases, purses and many other things.

One of the most amazingly useful woven items in Cambodia is the *krama* (pronounced kra-MAA). This is a piece of cloth, traditionally cotton or silk in a check pattern, about two metres long and half a metre wide. You often see it wrapped around someone's head and neck in a kind of turban style, as protection from the sun. This may show that the Khmer people originally came from India, as no other country in Southeast Asia wears the krama.

This scarf is used in dozens of different ways. You see mothers carrying their babies in their krama, or women hoisting live chickens to market. When wrapped like a turban, the scarf makes a good resting place if you want to carry a heavy basket on your head. It can be draped around your waist to make a skirt, or folded up and used as a pillow. If you want to carry a bottle of water, which you should in such a hot climate, you can wrap it in your krama and tie it around your waist.

Although Cambodians have known how to weave cloth for centuries, they need aid in making sure they get a good price for their products. Groups from outside the country come in, training people to make handicrafts and also helping them get fair wages. Others come in order to help improve life for villagers, for example, teaching the people how to grow crops in the best way or how to find clean drinking water. Still other organisations are there to make sure the people are treated justly, to aid the disadvantaged, to provide health care and education and for many other reasons.

These organisations from outside are called *non-governmental organisations* or NGOs. They are groups who do not represent any particular government, and in most cases are there simply to help. Many of these are charities which work with disabled people, women who have been mistreated or orphans.

Laura has been able to volunteer with one of these groups, called *Daughters*. In Cambodia, young women are sometimes sold by their families to people who treat them badly and make them do difficult work for little money. These women are like slaves. *Daughters* rescues such women, giving them a place to live and teaching them how to make eco-friendly handicrafts such as placemats and handbags. The women don't have to be slaves any more, because they can earn their own living. As they live in this caring environment, they gradually understand that God loves them and that they are very valuable as people.

Sophea was one person who was helped by an NGO. At age seventeen she married a man from her village. A few months later he told her they were moving to a distant province to find work. They arrived and checked into a guest house. Sophea's husband went off with some friends for the evening – and never came back. She had no idea where he was, and had no money to pay for her stay at the guest house. She didn't know anyone in the area.

Then the truth came out: her husband had sold her to the owner of the guest house! The man threatened to beat her if she didn't work for him. After three years of hard, humiliating work, Sophea cried out, 'If there is a God, help me please!'

Then one day someone came and paid money to the guest house owner for her. She was free! She went to live at an NGO project that helps women like this, and she came to know Jesus.

She also learned to read and was taught skills. Sophea was very ill when she arrived at her new home, and she only lived for three more years. But those three years were the happiest of her life.

These young women, sometimes referred to as 'vulnerable women', are slaves to other people. You may be shocked by that. But we are all slaves, in a way, before we come to know Jesus. We are not able to keep from doing wrong, and our hearts are cold to God. We are stuck. Yet, just as someone paid to set Sophea free, Jesus paid with his death, to set sinners free. Like the crafts Cambodians make out of discarded items, God wants to make something surprising and beautiful of every one of us, no matter what we are like. He delights in taking someone who is feeling empty and useless, and making them into a person who is full of his life and love.

If he has done that for you, have you told anyone? Your friends and family need to hear about our wonderful God. Pray for them. Ask God to give you a chance to talk to them, and the words to say. Pray that he will be working in their hearts, helping them want to know him. God is the one who saves, yet he uses people like you and me to spread the word. You may not know a lot, but you can tell someone else what God has done for you.

Laura gets excited about helping women in Cambodia to discover God's best for their lives. Part of her work has been training village women in basic principles of design and colour. For example, you probably know how to mix paint to make the colour green – you combine yellow and blue. The women Laura met had never heard of that before. She has also taught them how to draw designs based on typical Cambodian flowers such as the lotus, and to improve their weaving skills.

This has inspired her to start her own organisation called *Soteah*, which means 'kindness'. She wants to assist those who would be out of work or even shunned because of their disabilities. These disabled artisans belong to cooperatives, which means they also get to share in the profits from their work. And they have the pleasure of knowing they are making quality products which are sold at a fair price to people in the UK.

Hundreds of groups like this have come alongside to help Cambodia develop into a productive, healthy country. When I think of these groups, I think of God's Spirit. Just as the Kingdom of Cambodia needs helpers in order to grow and become strong, so Christians need help every day from the Holy Spirit, in order to be growing strong in our relationship with Jesus.

Sometimes people think that being a follower of Jesus means just trying to imitate Jesus. They ask, 'What would Jesus do in this situation?' and then try their best to do the same. But after a while they may get discouraged and give up. Jesus never intended for us simply to copy him. He gave his Spirit to live right inside us, helping us know when we're off track, and helping us to live in his way. When we let his Spirit guide us through each day, we will find ourselves more and more able to obey him in a way that brings joy to our lives.

We're coming to the end of our journey to Cambodia, this land full of amazing wildlife and fascinating people. Did you have a good trip? You may never get to travel to Cambodia in person, but I hope you have enjoyed being there in the pages of this book. Don't forget to pray for this country. Most of all pray for the people, that God will lead them out of darkness and fear of spirits. Pray that many will find their way to Jesus, the light of life.

Jesus says, 'If you love me, obey my commandments. And I will ask the Father, and he will give you another Counsellor, who will never leave you. He is the Holy Spirit, who leads into all truth.' (John 14:15-17)

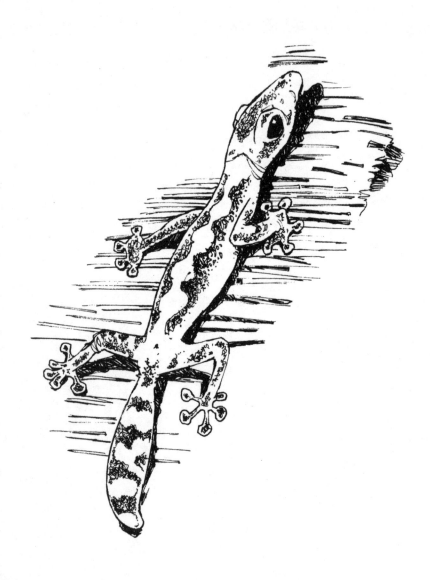

Map of Cambodia

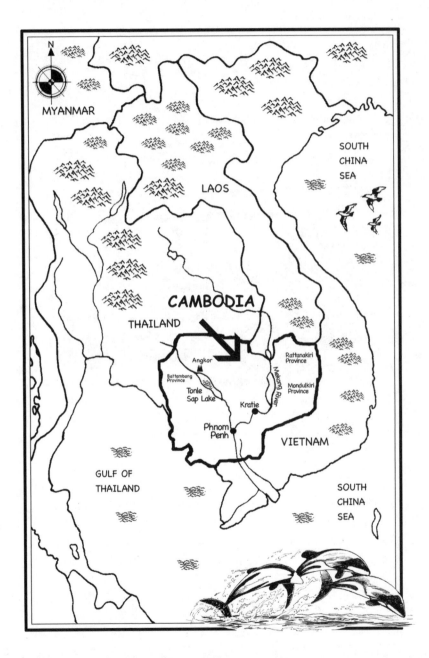

CAMBODIA QUIZ

1. What kind of musical entertainment is very popular in Cambodia?

2. Besides Cambodia, can you name the other countries of Southeast Asia?

3. What is the name of the roofed carriage pulled by a motorcycle?

4. What time in the morning do people get up in Cambodia?

5. What is the main religion of the country?

6. Why does milk have to be brought in from outside the country?

7. What provides electricity in a village house?

8. What is the main crop grown in Cambodia?

9. Why are water buffalo best for ploughing rice paddies?

10. What is unusual about the villages of Tonle Sap lake?

11. Which is the most dangerous snake in Cambodia?

12. What is the meaning of the word 'wat'?

13. How does the strangler fig tree get its name?

14. How do some poor children in Phnom Penh earn money?

15. What is a sweatshop?

16. How do kids play football in Cambodia?

17. How do we find out what God is like?

18. When do people celebrate becoming a year older?

19. What is an MDD trained to do?

20. How many minority groups in the world do not have the Bible in their own language?

21. How does a gecko walk on the ceiling?

22. What animal in Cambodia can you ride on?

23. What handicraft can you make with old magazines?

24. What kind of leaves does the silkworm eat?

25. Whose help do we need every day, in order to be growing strong in our relationship with Jesus?

26. What did Jesus do for us when he died on the cross?

27. What happens if we hold anger in our hearts?

28. What does *reconciliation* mean?

ANSWERS TO CAMBODIA QUIZ

1. Karaoke.

2. Vietnam, Thailand, Laos, Myanmar.

3. A tuk-tuk.

4. About 5 am.

5. Buddhism.

6. The cows are too scrawny.

7. A car battery.

8. Rice.

9. They have large padded hooves.

10. They are floating on the waters of the lake.

11. The Malayan pit viper.

12. Temple.

13. It takes root in another tree and squeezes the life out of it.

14. By picking through the city rubbish dump to find things to sell.

15. A clothing factory where children live and work long hours sewing garments.

16. Barefoot.

17. One way is by looking at Jesus.

18. During New Year, in April.

19. Sniff out land mines or unexploded weapons under the soil.

20. Nearly 3000.

21. Its feet are covered with tiny hairs.

22. The elephant.

23. Beads for jewellery.

24. Mulberry leaves.

25. The Holy Spirit.

26. He was punished for every wrong thing that his people have thought, said or done.

27. It turns into bitterness, which is very hard to get rid of.

28. Restoring a broken relationship.

ABOUT THE AUTHOR

Donna Vann always wanted to be a writer, because books meant so much to her when she was younger. She kept notebooks of her stories but did not begin writing books until she had three children of her own. Donna grew up in Texas. She and her husband work with an international Christian charity called Agapé Europe, and have lived in the UK for many years. She may be contacted via her website, www.donnavann.com

Look out for Wild West Adventures
also by Donna Vann

Other books by Donna Vann:

Corin's Quest:

ISBN:978-1-85792-218-9

Adventure and intrigue in Medieval England!
Exciting!
Dramatic! A Must Read!

King Arthur's Ransom

ISBN: 978-1- 85792 -849-5

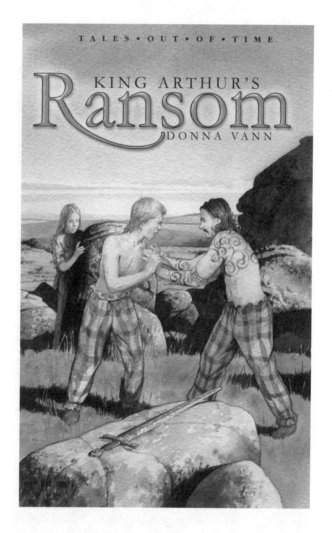

Adventure and danger in Bronze Age Britain!
Historical Fiction with Dramatic Energy.
Will young Arthur win the day?